Spherical Woman

Spherical Woman

Kysha Brown Robinson

New Orleans

Published by
Runagate Multimedia
P.O. Box 52723, New Orleans, LA 70152

Cover design by Lidya Araya
Cover art by Kysha Brown Robinson
Cover Photo by JR Thomason
Layout by Danielle Miles, odDbutCoMplete Designs

Copyright © 2009 Kysha Brown Robinson. All rights reserved.

Special Thanks to: The writers of NOMMO Literary Society and the Neo-Griot Workshop; my instructors and fellow workshop participants in the Low Residency Program at the University of New Orleans; Kalamu ya Salaam, Paulette Richards, Lynn Pitts, Karen Celestan, and Freddi Evans for your assistance with this collection. Special thanks to Danielle Miles for being an incredible friend, designer and project manager. Finally, my thanks to Fredrick, my favorite husband, a friend, a confidant, an inspiration – a very special love.

No part of this publication may be reproduced, stored in a retrieval system, or transmitted, in any form or by any means, electronic, mechanical, photocopying, recording, or otherwise, without prior permission of the author.

ISBN: 978-0-9653854-2-8
LCCN: 2009910136
Manufactured in the United States of America

For my big brother, Kenny,
who taught me to read and write.

Table of Contents

Memory/Gender/Geometry

a letter to my self	1
when lost, ask for directions	3
Lonely Women	5
of seeds and surrender	8
the question	9
brown girl blues	10
a song for serpents	13
close encounters	15
soon, again	17
Oshea 1	18
Oshea 2	19
Oshea 3	20
Oshea 4	21
canons don't come in peace	22
Poem for New Orleans	24
Survivors	26
fierce spherical woman	30
count it off	32
the corner market	34
vacancy	36
Dear Grandma	38
business class	40
Hindsight	42
Oshea 6	44
workin'	46
the core	48
something to show	50
epilogue	51
The Revealing Light of Honesty	62

Memory/Gender/Geometry

Poets who value language, tradition, and craft do not suffer anxiety of influence. They have absorbed the works of their literary ancestors and invest their talents in making innovations. Such a gifted poet is Kysha Brown Robinson. From her explorations in poetry and poetics, her journeys in the mindscape of African American women's poetry, she has gained insights about the elaboration of gendered perspectives. She has mastered those angles of imagination that bid us to acknowledge the complexity of human existence and acts of speech. In a time of ultra-technicality, Robinson is a poet who refuses to abandon the lasting pleasures of the page for the more immediate promises of the spoken word. Her poems negotiate a fine balance between the craftsperson's respect for language(s) and the engaged writer's commitment to raze the American house of disaffirming clichés and stereotypes. We find that balance in the voice of Hurricane Katrina survivors who are

overdosed on ironic surprise
hearth guard hatchet bearers
ascending steps and attic
stares from the rooftops
of ruins, we braved it
all to protect, and there
is nothing left
we are overdosed on charitized
eating sentiment-seasoned
complementaries, needing
levees and elevation planes
insurance meant to recompense
and one last claim
for justice

Just as Robert Moses, the legendary founder of the Algebra Project, recognized the centrality of math literacy in building a culture of change, Robinson recognizes how innovative geometric metaphors and images can be in the making of a poem. To be sure, her poems do not lack the sensuality that is so explicit in a line that suggests a woman might ride a man "from midnight to have mercy." On the other hand, the critical intelligence of her poetry is more essentially represented by a stanza from "fierce spherical woman"

I am
the directness of diameters
dissecting planes of desire
no matter where I be
I want to see
the other possibilities

This powerful assertion of identity is akin to and is a rememory of assertion in Mari Evans's signature poem "I Am A Black Woman" where the persona is "strong/beyond all definition still/ defying place/and time/and circumstance." The title of her collection, Spherical Woman, echoes Maya Angelou to the extent that the word "phenomenal has been shifted and replaced by "spherical." this re-entitlement moves us from celebration and awe to a geometrical articulation (or figuration) of intent. A reading of Robinson's poems through the lens of mathematical thought helps us to discover just how seriously her work seeks to renew us. Her method, which is her aesthetic, is grounded in manipulation of geometry and gender.

The poems in Spherical Woman urge us to be remote from the limits of two-dimensionality, the binary, and to ponder the properties of sphericality in motion, the surface and the interior, the area and the volume. Thus, in the opening poem " a letter to my self," the persona is deliberately split, alerting us to multiple states of being, to our reflexive conduct of everyday life. The poem's tone teases us into thought, preparing us for high moments of linguistic wit in "Survivors" or for the attention to number that sustains "Count it off."

Robinson explores familiar themes ---- family relationships, the doubts that occur in the intense moments of intimacy, expectations that may prompt women to repress breathing when the promise of the rainbow fails. Her forte, however, is performing quiet surgical operations on the anatomy of racism. Having been mentored by Kalamu ya Salaam, who himself was mentored by Tom Dent, Robinson is keenly aware that the most effective criticism in poetry is projected in concrete images. She is aware too that blues is an honored part of African American poetic tradition and has her rite of passage in the poems "Oshe 6" and "Brown Girl Blues." "Oshe 6" resonates the lyric postures of Ma Rainey, Bessie Smith, and Alberta Hunter. The version of "Brown Girl Blues" printed here is remarkably different from the poem of the same title published in the cross-generational anthology Catch the Fire!!! (1998). The current version is more dramatic and expressed with greater economy of means. Comparing the two versions gives us a better sense of the Kysha Brown Robinson who is now in contrast to the Kysha N. Brown who was then.

Spherical Woman is a powerful invitation to share one woman's critical engagement with language and the geometry of everyday life in America.

Jerry W. Ward, Jr.
December 20, 2008

a letter to my self

FROM:
the me i am
in this space & time

TO:
the me i want to be
in my own tomorrows

dear me

i am
writing
to say
that i am finally
ready
to join
you
in our
future

it has taken me
so long
to disembark
because
packing our bags
for life
is no easy task

at first
i let me pack things
we do not need

a duffel
for my uncle's niece

carry-on
for my lover's lady
pullman
for my siblings' sister
trunk
for my parents' daughter
all more than we
can carry

as i and i both know
whatever the means of transport
there is always a cost
for excess baggage

after reconsidering
necessity
i decreased the load
to one
backpack

at any rate
i'm headed our way
take care
i'll be you
when i get there

∎

when lost, ask for directions

I.
how can we
end this tale

of two cities
on a map
with a scale surreal
where a few inches
between father and daughter
equal a million miles

with small hands
fingers short like yours
I could trace
the line of your nose
and know
my own reflection

but these days
we touch
without feeling

I could look
into your eyes
and see myself
but even at our closest
we stand
back to back

II.
each time you left us
for letters
behind
your name
I learned to forget
that I loved you

each time
you returned
wiser of the world
to a household
of unlettered strangers

while you defended
your dissertation
I was bullied
on bus 29

but I guess that was not
your committee's concern

III.
I am
your failures
and aspirations

can you love yourself
enough
to know me

can we, daddy
mourn these miles
and cry cry
a river
'til we fill our canyon

and let love
cruise 'cross
on a raft
of reconciliation

■

Lonely Women

we are fatherless daughters
entering womanhood
with only half our selves
worshipping the mystique
of masculinity

naked bodies flying
willingly
over the edge
of countless cliffs
praying the god of gravity
will grant us grace

you see us at parties
getting drunk on emptiness
dancing dirty with strangers
or worse -- with men we know

we will do what we don't
to please our lovers
'cause this one could be
the one
our hearts hold
scrap
books
full of faded photographs
of the faces
of could have been

we marry money
for security
become servants
in master bedrooms
and wake up in dream homes

turned nightmare insanitoria
where we are ex-wives
wondering when
love disembarked
the journey to death us do part

we are patient predators
in pitiable holding patterns
vultures in friendship's camouflage
who pick the meat from marriages

we are tits and asses
flaunting form
fitted fashions
so when a man comes our way
he can see good reason to stay

we are new and improved
women, working out
toning up
slimming down
laying on the hippest beaches
at the hottest getaways
under the sun-bright spotlight
praying that some bronze brother
will have cause to pause
long enough to discover that
we can whip up gourmet soul food
help meet the mortgage
watch sports all day on Sunday
and ride him from midnight
to have mercy
and we are women of our word

women with it going on
plenty of papers and props

driving fancy cars to fine homes
that we share with our
parents
children
fantasies
fingertips

we are lonely women
waiting for someone
to want us
wanting someone
to need us
needing
someone

∎

of seeds and surrender

I mix emotions and mold the dust
Of your pulverized bones into skeletons
Dancing in the closet of my regrets

I cloak your frames in the flesh of fantasy
And imagine all you could have been
Some days are dark and dank
As the walls of my vacuumed womb
Some nights flooded with the blinding light
Of internal interrogations

Do my choices make me a woman unworthy
Of respect, of love, of happiness?
Should a bomb or bullet bear my name
Or bareness befall me?

I am without answers
As I am without you
The seeds I sacrificed
To save a self

I could not surrender
■

the question

"do you love me," she asked
but what she really wanted
to know was
if he thought
she was beautiful

"do you love me," she asked
but what she really wanted
to know was
if he considered
his relationship with her
more important
than all others

"do you love me," she asked
but what she really wanted
to know was
if he could deal
with her idiosyncrasies

"do you love me," she asked
but what she really wanted
to know was
if he promised fidelity

"do you love me," she asked
"of course I love you," he answered

she would spend a lifetime
wondering
if he really
understood
the question

∎

brown girl blues

I had imagined you
brown to the bone

mahogany lifeblood
moving through your veins

and I really liked brown
black boys with chestnut hands

even your nails
were brownish tan

you had to be
brown to the bone

I dreamt purple passion
and private pleasures

received them as gifts
in our daylight realities

exploding into crimson cries
for more always more, then

my curiosity craved delight
until that morning when....

I knocked on your door, baby
but I didn't hear no sound

tap, tap, tapped on your door
and I didn't hear no sound
but I kept on tapping
cuz I knew you wuz around

you finally said, "who is it?"
and all I said was, "me"
I heard you ask, "who is it?"
and I said that it was me
that's how I always answered
cuz baby who else would it be?

you opened the door just a little
like I was someone you didn't know
and you talked to me
through that crack in your door
I had to bust in baby
to see what you wuz hiding for

it was like a black hole
horror movie matinee

my eyes raging red
floodlighting your infidelity

I tried to flee the seen
of your depravity

but you followed
in pitiful pageantry

you said, "listen baby
this really isn't what it seems"
tried to tell me
it really wasn't what it seemed
that your brown bones wuzn't
boning someone other than me

but eyes had heard
all there was to say
I hurried to my car
holding my heart in place
and searching for the key to freedom

in the bottom of my bag
you shrank to nothing
in my rear view mirror
shrank to nothing
on my heart's horizon

drivin' up that highway
sho' nuff feelin' down and low
drivin' down that highway
I was feelin' mighty low
man you know'd I loved you
why'd you have to be a 'ho'?

■

a song for serpents

I.
I see you my brother
in your slimy, snakish ways
hissing unity and revolution
while your tail is wrapped
around your mother's neck
   having forgotten the days
   her heart was your attic

I hear even your closet talk
gang bang gossip of secret seductions
sleeping with sisters you don't respect

I must remind you
that lucifer is your slave name

relive the day
of your beautifully black
birth, sacred serpent
gliding from
earth mother womb
into a world wondering
what to do
with your serpentine smooth

shed
your shady ways
be the new

rejuvenation
of your self

Haiti called you Damballah
crawling out of worn ways
away from shackles
of oppression

biting your tail
and becoming
the never-endinng
circle of life

II.
let us be we
a caduceus of our colony
in this oppressive land
as the healers knew
it takes two intertwined
in body and mind
head to head
and tail to tail

we will make mistakes
being snakes trying to awaken
a revolution in our people
but we must keep trying

must glide out of and beyond
our indiscretion

and keep on pushing

must make earth
mama so proud
that she will smile rivers
and cry tributaries
inspiring our every undulation

as we
contract
as we
expand
as we
move
as we
change
∎

close encounters

I.
exposure
we stood
in the midst of
music and emotion
the soft rise
of my cheek pressed
against your bare chest
fingers curled up and
over your shoulders

in a rare moment
I undressed my soul
exposed my need
but you did not recognize
my nakedness
and wondered why
I only removed my shoes

II.
rapture
you furled
your frame
down
and around
I was cloaked
and caressed
with kisses
and uncertainty
I did not know
which was more
immense
the passion
of your touch
or the depth
of my need

III.
crossing
your lips dance
across the bridge
of my hips swaying
with the tremulous pulse
of your pleasured
purrrrr
your heart beats
a talking drum
to which I respond racing
toward your rhythm
'til my feet reach safety
one cradled
in the small of your back
the other nestled
in the bend
just behind
your knee deep
in the river now

yes, we are in the river
baptized in warm baths
tongues touch tenderness
feather fingers and finesse
where nothing matters

but this moment
our crossing
each breath
this moment
crossing
until I lay
on the bank of your broadness
arms outstretched
in the sweetness
of our salty dew

∎

soon, again

anticipating your caress

I lie facing the door

and smile wet kisses

in secret spaces

∎

Oshea 1

You travel the direction of your dreams
and I mine

You cross mountains and lakes
down the river line
bank to bank and back again
over canyon, desert plain
from ocean to opposite shore

My meanderings circle back
to meet old faces
always going, but never leaving

I belong somewhere
You, everywhere

And we are
together
getting there

■

Oshea 2

how can two who love
live so far apart?

we fill our in between with knowing
your mississippi music crossing
three times on wanting and whisperings

do miles really equal distance?
proximity closeness?

at the river's lip I sit
listening for soon come somedays
and our peach sweet reunion

■

Oshea 3

ours is not the dance
of ocean and shoreline
far less flow than ebb

both immersed and asunder
a handholding stroll
without touch

except
your heart beating
against my forever

except
the scent of my hair
wrapped around
your recollection

∎

Oshea 4

as you open
your arms to me

I fill your embrace
with the absence of need
∎

canons don't come in peace

artillery intent on domination
weapons of annihilation
canons don't come in peace

a shot over the bow warns us
but the ocean is bleeding

we gaze through our ruddy reflections
through the dust of our ancestors' bones
and bear witness to the seafloor's wounds

who will defend our water?
who will defend our woods?

there were war cries
before weeping on the trail of tears
canons smashed the essence of existence

natives labeled savages
rain forests called jungles

the destruction is devastating
the deathblows deafening
the stench of oppression pervades the air
shrapnel shreds our eyes
can we see the truth?
projectiles pierce our tongues
can we speak the truth?

who will defend our waters?
who will defend our woods?
who will defend our world?
who will defend us who ain't white
and don't have dicks?

targets marked
with scarlet letters
a shot over the bow
of the mother
ship
she kept coming, she kept coming
he used more accurate artillery
and blew off her head
bullets in her womb

father son no mother
father son no mother
father son no mother
jesus, is your mama really a ghost
in the aftermath of war?

will we defend our waters?
will we defend our woods?
will we defend our world?
will we defend us who ain't white
and don't have dicks?

∎

Poem for New Orleans

When first eye
Saw the city
She was
Indians, krewes
Red sauce, roux
Jazz, blues
Voodoo and Jesus, too

A hallowed whorehouse
Where brothers greet guests curbside
Hands too helpful
Smiles too wide
Welcome to the city
Where every mayor
Is just another madam
Trying to pay the mortgage
To the man

And they came crawling
From cave and countryside
Daily, by tens of thousands
Suburban parasites
With carnivorous cravings
Came proclaiming her
Den of sin
Mecca of murder
But still they came
To suck her blood
And breast milk
To feast upon her flesh

By tens of thousands
A daily retreat
Bellies full
Pockets bulging

What prayer,
What panacea?
To save this dying woman
Who lies helpless
Between a pool of tears
And a river of blood

∎

Survivors

standing in the checkout line

the sister in front of me
pulls out a brand new book of food stamps

and eyes from all directions
cashier
bagboy
white people in line behind me

though not the white woman in the next line
who softly whispers
"this will be with stamps"

but eyes from all other directions

piercing
cutting
slashing
stabbing this sister
maiming her self pride
murdering her self-esteem
mutilating her self-respect

then I hear whispers behind me
the whispers you hear
when you know people are talking about you
but are too scared to say that shit out loud

whispers

"reform"
"work like the rest of us"
"laying up making babies"

"and this one...
who me?
...probably has those damn food stamps too"

and i/we turned around

me and my feet
tired from working two jobs
to pay my half of the ghetto rent
me and my momma's back
strong from picking a bale of cotton a day
in the fields of south carolina
me and my grandmomma's fingers
twisted from sewing white folks clothes
and clothes for their children
who called her by her familiar name
me and my great grandmomma's womb
once tender from giving birth one morning
then returning to the field that same afternoon

we all turned around in the checkout line that night

we are four generations
of government subsidy supporting southern belles
slavery was an endless book of food stamps for slave owners

a satanic system that grew fat on food
planted by African hands
harvested by African hands
prepared by African hands
served by African hands
to masters and mistresses of hatred and oppression
who gave thanks to sky gods
for the sweat blood bounty of the earth
sat at tables of plenty
that they had the audacity to call their own
while servant slaves stood

and waited
and worked
and waited

and i'm still standing
in the checkout line at winn dixie
wishing dixie hadn't won
where southern belles lived in section 8 plantation houses
that damn sure didn't look like the projects

so maybe sisters on welfare
maybe sisters using food stamps
should start referring to themselves as
genteel southern ladies
maybe they should start identifying themselves
as what they truly are
survivors of war

sister-soldiers, stronger bolder
we are survivors
of educational concentration camps disguised as schools
that provide us with still separate and unequal opportunity
load our mind guns with intellectual blanks
and march us to the front lines of the workforce
to be gunned down by part-time no-time hard-times
survivors of the constant flurry of lies and misrepresentations
fired from the automatic image weapons
of television networks and music mogul conglomerates
aimed at assassinating the realities of
African families in america

survivors of the systematic destruction of our familihoods
survivors of covert and overt racism of today

we are survivors and the descendants of survivors
of the war against our civil rights
the post-reconstruction holocaust
and slavery in america

we are descendants of survivors
of the colonization of our mothers
the colonization of the motherland
and the colonization of the planet
that we are alive is a victory

the cashier
still not recognizing the sister
as the survivor that she was
asked, "will that be with food stamps?"

the sister closed her eyes
looked into the mirror of her soul
saw herself
her mother
her grandmother
great grandmother
great-great grandmother
kissing white asses generation after generation
and she can't even use her stamps to buy toilet paper
with which to wipe her own

sister soldier felt the eyes
piercing
cutting
slashing
stabbing

"will that be with food stamps?"

she took a deep breath, smiled and said
for herself, for all of us

"No, I'll be paying with reparations."

∎

fierce spherical woman

in a world of squares
I spin thirds
entrapped in cubicles
plotting the means
to the arc of my dreams

I am
the directness of diameters
dissecting planes of desire
no matter where I be
I want to see
the other possibilities

a body celestial
life light of day
moon's passion bright
dancing the fidelity
of earth

I come 'round the
bend without fear
of the unseen
'cause you can't be
a woman
'less you can
handle curves

I am
a fierce spherical woman
bringing the arc of love
to the lithosphere

■

Bill Huntington
(jazz master)

made

the

bass

moan

fingered her pain
scroll to end pin
to scroll again

heaving woe
from the hollowed bridge
of her belly. my tear
drops turned on her dirge
my own mourning

improvisation merged maple
and melancholy. unlocked my spirit
gates overflowing with all the sadness
I had ever known.
Bill Huntington
made the bass.
moan

■

count it off

at the corner store, it's two by two
whole time the cashier watches you
the price is twice what it costs for one
you pay it quick, and the next two come

the clinic books us three by three
rush us through, get the Medicaid fee
cancel us out if we dare come late
packed in a room we wait and wait

with four of us, police see trouble
"gimme that corner," they're not so subtle
we don't meet the profile, it meets us
so we move along without a fuss
we move along without a fuss

■

13 January 2004
I penciled the original version of this poem on a notebook I keep on my bedside table. Then I typed the second version in my laptop. The inspiration came as I stopped at the corner of Jackson Avenue and Oretha Castle Haley Boulevard. A teenager was managing a group of younger kids who wanted to buy snacks at the corner store. She was explaining to a few newcomers that they had to wait their turn because the owners only allow two kids at a time to enter the store..

the corner market

at the corner market
today's special
buy some
get none free
■

28 January 2004
written in pencil in the
notebook which now sits on the bed.
the pens and pencils are
still on the bedside table (lest I mark
the linens). I awoke around
5:30 am to "dictate"
these lines.

the lines below were
once at the beginning
of the poem. now they
are here on the cutting
room floor...

it is agreed
a handshake
an afternoon's fortune
for a few moments
without memory
yes?
yes

it is agreed
a parting of flesh
for what
might have been
brotherly benevolence
yes?
yes

vacancy

it lands
on a small, but able limb
left by another
collects bits of fallen leaf
blades of grass
broken pine needles
now brown and better
for the weave
repairs the small nest
here now is home
a space ordered its own

■

02 February 2004
9:10 am
typed on laptop
at home in Schaumburg
sitting on the bed
lines of light through the blinds
cars passing
birds chirping
they fly across the landscape of snowcover
I imagine birds from my childhood
claiming nests in our front yard

Dear Grandma

I watched you peel away
your elegance to suit your mornings
spent kneeling before rows of beans
or standing between stalks of corn
only a small brim and simple smock
between you and the burden
of the summer sun, between you
and its beauty, too
I want elegant words
for this remembrance
I want, even now,
to earn your smile

■

06 February 2004
7:30 a.m.
lying in bed
black pen from bedside table
written on the front of the same
9 x 12 envelope from last night
typed version is a revision
of handwritten notes
and includes some lines
from the back of the envelope

I can't remember when
I wrote those lines

business class

catches the days first flight
his affairs are most important

leaves the snow of home
to land in New Orleans

rises, attaché case in hand
removes his overcoat

from the overhead compartment
an item he won't need here

his wedding band now
in his left pants pocket

∎

11:40 pm. 07 February 2004
sitting on the bed
in the Doubletree Houston
My friend and mentor
with whom I attended a seminar today
sits on her bed reading some papers
poem inspired by a guy I sat next to
on the flight from ORD to MSY on Tuesday
I originally typed some notes to remind me
of the moment of inspiration at 1:23pm on Tuesday
I sat down to review the notes. the poem arrived
during the review

Hindsight

My young eyes
could not discern happiness
hidden by years of everyday
duties varied only by seasons
some days planting
some pruning
others the harvest
all rise to work
bend and rise
rest, rise
your joy was always
there I'm certain now
as mine now glimmers
beneath the weight
of my own routine

■

24 February 2004
12:52 PM
on the flight
ATL to MSY
typed on my laptop
formed from notes
written in my blue notepad
I just finished typing in
two poems I wrote this morning

these notes I wrote
while waiting in the doctor's office
12 February 2004
early afternoon

thinking a lot lately
about my grandmother
Lydia Martin
Lydia M. Brown

Oshea 6

since you been gone away
there ain't nobody sawin'
since you been gone my love
nobody choppin' wood
with all that nighttime quiet
thought I'd be sleepin' good

say love it don't get lost
gets home dark or light
say love don't get lost baby
finds home dark or light
bring home your rowdy ruckus
and take this silent night

I'm tossin' turnin' yearnin'
you ain't here next to me
I'm tossin' turnin' yearnin'
my man ain't next to me
it says I got the queen size
the king I need to see

■

17 February 2004
9:56 pm
sitting on the futon
typing on the laptop
still missing my husband

1 May 2004
I changed a line in the first stanza
to be certain I included
the cliché of sawing logs
for the sake of clarity

workin'

                        control the labor force

                        cajole the labor force

                        chokehold the labor force

                        console the labor force

                        who **stole** the labor force

                        who **sold** the labor force

                        who **rolled** the labor force

                        control the labor force

                                                  ■

27 February 2004
12:14 am

I'm sitting in bed
in an upstairs bedroom
in my host's home
in this quaint Louisiana town
a georgous place on the river
it's been an entire day of meetings
then working for a few minutes

I can get a few hours sleep
then it's back to New Orleans
and more meetings
the poem inspired by several things

the extreme wealth and poverty here
my host's honesty
about her family's wealth
the wealth of her friends and neighbors

conversation with a new acquaintance

our afternoon tour
of the other side of town

my family history

i pray my ancestors
(my elders, too)
don't come and choke me in the night
for sleeping in the big house
1 May 2004
restored font size
as I prepared Spring 2004 manuscript

the core

when they operate in your abdomen
you discern the dancer's truth
the debutante's mantra as she descends
the stair.

        it's
           all
              in
                  your
                      center

you find your legs
machines without power
'til you rebuild your belly's strength
each rediscovered ability
an achievement without the fanfare
of a baby's firsts

■

15 April 2004
3:54 am
this morning I learned
to use the strength of my arms
grab the tightly tucked sheet
and pull myself up just a little
at least enough
to tilt my head
and look at the pages
of this binder
and write these words
in black ink

I am consumed with my body
with healing
with the medicine
with food
with rest
with meditations
and prayers
actually, that is all lies
I'm just high
on pain meds
oh my
time to ration
before depleting
my supply
1 May 2004
added the word "belly's"
~~still not satisfied~~
~~in process~~
moving on

something to show

looking back
some lines of the work
that got created
that I created
stand out for me

a long walk
a never bow down
rediscovered ability
an achievement
without fanfare

my friends said
they like some of the notes
more than some of the poems
I do, too
so I choose this note to close

I have seen new approaches
expanded my writing community
discovered innovators
of many of the tools I use

I wrote my way
through travels
literal and symbolic
I am up and about again
I know myself newly
more write, less rewrite

this was a season
claiming its own name
∎

Epilogue
the Katrina poems

SOS

if i answer the call
of trumpet sound
dance beneath the sea
am buried
my feet above the ground
somebody pray for me

What I brought

I.
Clean drawz, three pair
Two bras, not the best
Black pants
Brown outfit
Green suit
Two shirts
White blouse
Stockings
Buba
Toiletries – the abbreviated version
Dressy brown shoes
Cell phone
PDA
Two laptops
Portable printer
Paper
3 phone batteries
Phone charger
All three debit cards
Two credit cards
AAA card
Medical insurance card
Two cases of water
All in my black Subaru

Next time I'll add
Two copies of each book we published
Five fabulous outfits, clean or not – cause the
media ain't friendly to negroes and laundromats and dry
cleaners be everywhere
Running shoes – 'cause sometimes you be runnin'
All my pretty drawz and good bras, clean or not – see
previous explanation

All my Chester Allen jewelry designs
Important documents
Shoes – at least six pair

II.
When you know you are all you got
That there are people who care about you
And would do whatever they could for you
Would give generously to the cause of you
But what you got now is one hour
Before contraflow forces you west or north
And ain't no time to request or receive generosity
When you know you are all you got
You pack the first stuff that comes to mind

You call Carol back and make sure
She got a way out
'Cause you regret the cross-eyed look you gave
When she said maybe she would come with you
And what was that look?
A betrayal she recognized
And you shame
But it's done now, now it's done
And she got her own way, thanks for nothin'
And you call some others
And they got a way
Those that answer

And you coulda took somebody with you
But you didn't
Didn't even ask
nobody who mighta really needed
A way
Out
Just left with what you had

You and the other haves
When you are all you got
And them that's not
got left

run

(the second leg of my NO,LA evacuation)

You got to escape for your life
Bright angels above
Sometimes escape for your life
Bright angels above

I am listening to Sweet Honey in the Rock. They are singing Run Mourner Run. I have driven through the northern half of Georgia, Tennessee, and Kentucky, and I am making my way through Indiana. At this point in the journey, it seems to take forever to get to the next state line. My mother calls to check on my progress, "Hey, what are you doing?"
"Watching the corn grow in Indiana." We laugh together. I want her to think I'm in good spirits. I don't tell her that I cried when I left her and Kim in Phenix City, Alabama. Even though she tells me how the two of them cried together, I want her to know that I am fine. I am always fine. Even in the midst of chaos I take on being "just fine" until I am. She ends our brief conversation with encouragement. I love my mother.
In eleven hours I drive 753 miles, including five stops for gas, restroom breaks, snacks, leg stretching, and sanity checks.

When I left New Orleans, I packed as if I were going away for the weekend. I fully expected to be home in two days – four at the most. Now I don't know when I will be allowed to return. I am clear that escaping for your life is not escaping with your life. My life in New Orleans is gone. I had called Mahmud earlier. I took issue with him referring to me as a refugee. "I'm not insulting you," he said, "I know what it is to be a refugee. On my passport it says STATELESS." I yelled back, "Well, that's you and your passport. I am an American citizen." I think to myself…for all that buys you if you're stuck in the Superdome or the Convention Center. I know that I was arguing technicality over reality. But with so many miles more to drive, arguing occurred as a useful activity in passing the time.

I am not stateless. But when I look at where I was in the Tremé and where I'm going in the Village of Schaumburg in the northwest suburbs of Chicago, it's clear that I was in another country. In its culture, New Orleans was not America. In some ways, New Orleans was not even Louisiana. Perhaps that's why it took so long for anyone to rescue people who could not or did not evacuate before the hurricane. I don't have answers or even much understanding – only images of what it is to be abandoned –in a crowd – in your own country.

■

Call me

when the birds stand perched
On the power line
by my balcony in Tremé

call me

when water returns
to its toxic norm
when a shower is ok

call me

when I can walk to the river
meet friends for coffee
no vigilantes 'long the way

when it's home again
soldiers gone again
just me and my neighbors
around the way

■

blues from the aftermath

Storm blew down through history
And whisked my life away
Flood crashed the levee
And washed my life away
Out here a thousand miles
From my home in the Tremé

somebody sing a dirge for me
a slow respectful stroll
somebody sing a dirge
for this dove on shoulder stroll
out here so far away
from the streets that know my soul

Ain't no second line
On this Sunday afternoon
No second line parade
On this Sunday afternoon
Ain't no brass band comin'
no buckjump no time soon

Georgia peach turned gumbo girl
Now meets the Midwest moon
Georgia peach turned crawfish queen
Beneath the Midwest moon
Will meet you on St. Claude
One Sunday 'fore next June

Can't say if just a visit
Or a journey home to stay
Can't say if just to visit
Or a journey home to stay
There's just one thing for certain
We'll dance another day
We'll step through the Tremé
We'll dance these blues away

■

Flying Home

blue-topped boxes
dot block after block

a boneyard
of fallen trees
form a pit of limbs

a batallian
of discarded dominoes
stand at putrid attention
like dualing keyboards
back to back to back

could we play
some levee break blues
or post-Katrina funk
so unbearably funky
we would strap each box
shut with a double belt
of duct
tape
record this moment
with appropriately
archaic technology
for this cacophony
of insufficiencies

I shake my head
and tighten the belt
for safe landing
and disconsolate arrival

∎

o.d.

we have overdosed on being wise
the road weary horde
heeding the call
cramped and crowded
in shelters, hotels and homes of hosts
who believed it would be just
a few days

we have overdosed on criticized
the overbaked rescued
stranded and starved
on interstates and in decimated halls
of unconventional unconcern

overdosed on ironic surprise
hearth guard hatchet bearers
ascending steps and attic
stares from the rooftops
ruins, we braved it
all to protect, and there
is nothing left

we are overdosed on charitized
eating sentiment-seasoned
complementaries, needing
levees and elevation planes
insurance meant to recompense
and one last claim
for justice

■

after words

The Revealing Light of Honesty

I know these poems. Was there when many of them were born.

Better yet, I know the poet. Was there when she wrote in halting block letters on lined paper and hoped for writer's fame and fortune. She showed me her hopes, dreams, the buds of her self-revelations. Shy she was. Her boyfriend asked me what I thought.

Characteristically unsemtimental, I simply replied: it's writing.

What I meant, and continue to mean, is it's one thing to write words, something else again to write the truth of one's life.

The poet heard me. Threw the arguments out the window, let the artificial light of opinions and surface feelings fade and began to work in the inner glow that is the revealing light of honesty.

If you listen closely you will hear both the noise and the music, the pain when a feeling is ripped loose from the flesh and pinned to the page, the esctasy when a song's joy sprung not from the throat but the heart and given new form as a poem.
I really like the would have been inherent in all those poems about missings. Missing a child that was but never breathed, a man that came but left, a father who sired but never surrendered to love's domestic chains or maybe that is all some love ever was: a surrender. Never a triumphant march through the city of self, arm and arm sailing the seas of life experiences.

I know her up close and have seen her at a distance. Once when we worked all night on a poetry project, she slept briefly on the office floor, contented as a kitten, bliss-filled in her exhaustion. When she married, I journeyed to Georgia, deep into the innards of lost/found, past Waycross out where the pine trees and the crows on fences inspect each stranger, just to be there and amen her "I do"—and I am not even a Christian. But I was there not to agree or bless, but to bear kinship witness, after all we wordsmiths must stick together or we will separate alone.

Yes, I know these poems and though I know I recognize in these words some things the common reader will never see, I also know that in the uncommon honesty of these words strangers will come and be shocked to recognize some things about themselves they thought were secrets.

There are no real secrets in life: only truths we try to hide but which a tear, a smile, a touch, a sibling or an unborn, a lover or task undone always reveals. For finally we are more than our faults, less than our grand accomplishments—we are ships on life's ocean, seeking, searching for human berth.

And this book is a captain's journal.

—Kalamu ya Salaam

Acknowledgements

My thanks to the editors of the following journals and anthologies in which some of these poems have appeared:

"A Song for Serpents." Beyond the Frontier: African-American Poetry for the 21st Century. Ed. E. Ethelbert Miller. Baltimore: Black Classic Press, 2002. 505-507.

"Survivors." Role Call. Ed. Tony Medina et al. Chicago: Third World Press, 2002. 51-53.

"When Lost Ask for Directions." Role Call. Ed. Tony Medina et al. Chicago: Third World Press, 2002. 183.

"Oshea 1-4." Black Magnolias. 2002.1:2.46-47.

"Lonely Women." bum rush the page: a def poetry jam. Eds. Tony Medina and Louis Reyes Rivera. New York: Three Rivers Press. 2001. 7-8.

"Crossing." heart-shaped vox. Ed. Andrei Codrescu and Dave Brinks. New Orleans: Gambit Weekly, 2000. 21:6.24.

"A Letter to Myself." The BlackWords Compilation Volume I: Jazz Poetry Kafe. BlackWords, Inc. 1999.

"When Lost, Ask For Directions." 360° A Revolution of Black Poets. Ed. Kalamu ya Salaam. Alexandria: BlackWords, 1998. 31-33.

"Nudity." 360° A Revolution of Black Poets. Ed. Kalamu ya Salaam. Alexandria: BlackWords, 1998. 34.

"Fierce Spherical Woman." 360° A Revolution of Black Poets. Ed. Kalamu ya Salaam. Alexandria: BlackWords, 1998. 35.

"Brown Girl Blues." Catch the Fire. Ed. Derrick I.M. Gilbert. New York: Riverhead Books, 1998. 128-130.

"A Letter to Myself." From a Bend in the River. Ed. Kalamu ya Salaam. New Orleans: Runagate Press, 1998. 30-31.

"Soon Again." Dark Eros. Reginald Martin. New York: St. Martin's Press, 1997. 177.

"Survivors." Fertile Ground - Memories & Visions. Ed. Kalamu ya Salaam and Kysha N. Brown. New Orleans: Runagate Press, 1996. 99-102.

"Canons Don't Come in Peace." Fertile Ground - Memories & Visions. Ed. Kalamu ya Salaam and Kysha N. Brown. New Orleans: Runagate Press, 1996. 118-119.

www.ingramcontent.com/pod-product-compliance
Lightning Source LLC
Chambersburg PA
CBHW051702090426
42736CB00013B/2497